Dear Coloring Book Enthusiast,

Thank you so much for purchasing my book!

My team and I have worked hard to make a great book for you. I hope you enjoying coloring it as much as we enjoyed making it.

I have a surprise for you...

This book includes a **free digital copy** (PDF format) so you can print your favorite images and color them an unlimited number of times.

Make sure to visit my website, **JadeSummer.com** to access:

- Image previews of every book
- Free bonus content (including coloring pages)
- Exclusive offers and book giveaways
- Links to Jade Summer on social media
- Finished coloring pages from our community
- Free "review copies" of new releases
- And much more!

Yours Truly,

Jade Summer

P.S. Do you know someone who would enjoy this book? Buy them a copy and make it a surprise gift. I promise they'll love it!

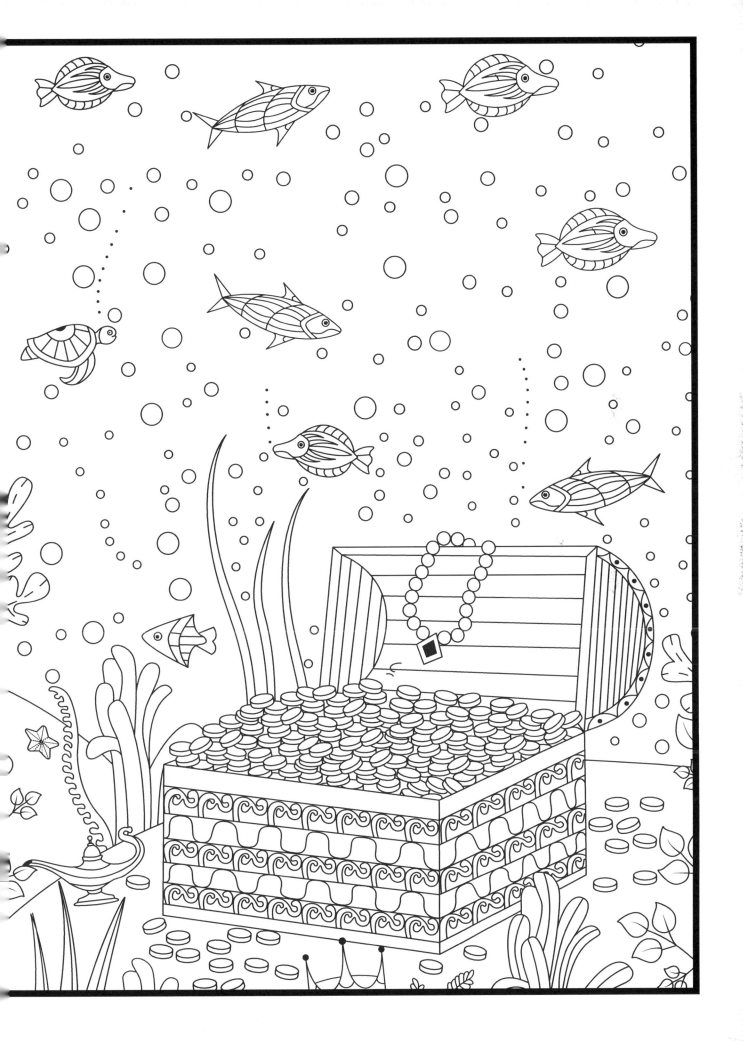

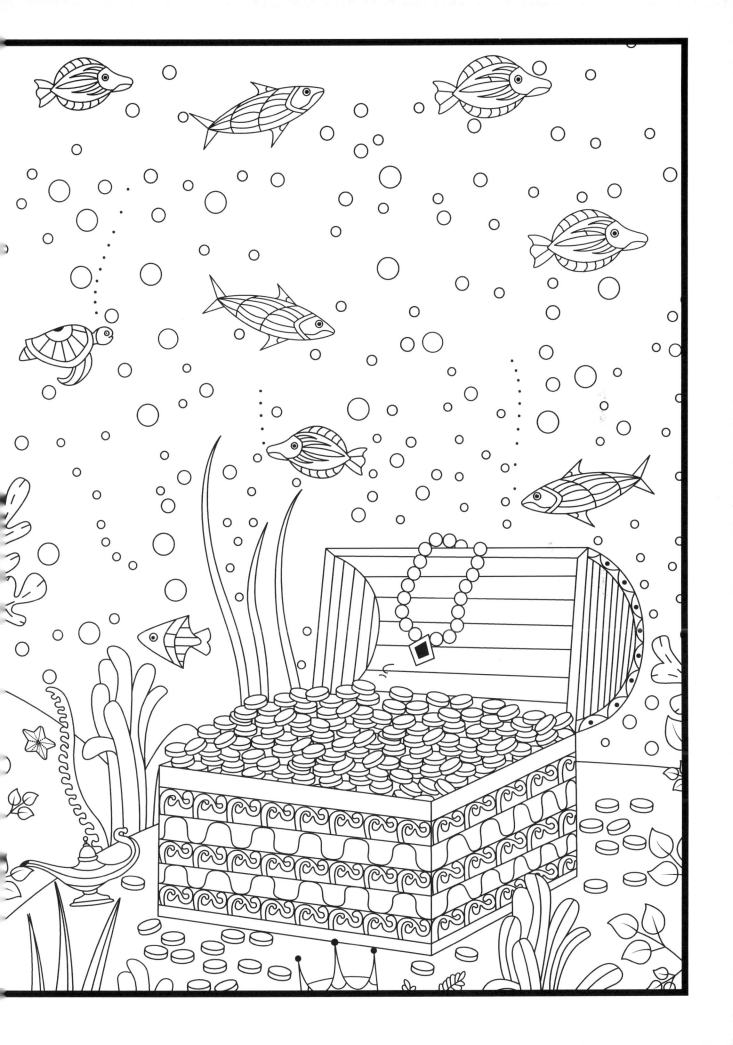

LEAVE MY AMAZON REVIEW

1. Go to Amazon
2. Search for *Jade Summer*
3. Find this book
4. Click the *Write a Review* button

JOIN US ON FACEBOOK

Facebook.com/JadeSummerColoring

Share your artwork, view artwork from other customers, and win free coloring books.

DOWNLOAD MY PDF VERSION

Go to **JadeSummer.com** and provide us with:

Title: **Under the Sea - Volume 1**
Access Code: **94U8M58Q**

Made in the USA
Middletown, DE
31 December 2016